BASKETBALL

BY KARA L. LAUGHLIN

The Child's World®

childsworld.com

Published by The Child's World®
1980 Lookout Drive • Mankato, MN 56003-1705
800-599-READ • www.childsworld.com

ACKNOWLEDGMENTS
The Child's World®: Mary Swensen, Publishing Director
The Design Lab: Design
Heidi Hogg: Editing
Sarah M. Miller: Editing

PHOTO CREDITS
© Aspenphoto/Dreamstime.com: 10; Aspen Photo/Shutterstock.com: 4, 9, 15, 20-21; Chris Minor/Shutterstock.com: 19; Debby Wong/Shutterstock.com: 13; Duplass/Shutterstock.com: 16; Eric Broder Van Dyke/Shutterstock.com: 6-7; Naypong/Shutterstock.com: 2-3; Sjankauskas/Dreamstime.com: cover, 1

ISBN: 9781503807716
LCCN: 2015958117

Printed in the United States of America
Mankato, MN
June, 2016
PA02300

TABLE OF CONTENTS

4

Game Time!

A **tip-off** starts the game. Two players face each other—one from each team.

The **ref** throws the ball high. Both players jump. Who will get the ball?

Baskets

The team with the ball runs to the other team's basket. The team works together. They try to get the ball in the other team's basket.

Fast Fact!
Each basketball team has five players.

Dribbling

In basketball, you run a lot! You must bounce the ball with one hand as you run. This is called **dribbling**.

You can also **pass**. To pass, you throw the ball to a teammate.

But be careful! The other team will try to **steal** the ball. If they do, they can take the ball and dribble it the other way.

Fast Fact!
You can also pass by bouncing the ball to a teammate.

11

Making Baskets

When the ball goes through the **net**, it is a **basket**. Most baskets are worth two points.

A **layup** is one way to shoot a basket. You run and jump. You throw the ball while you are in the air.

Fast Fact!
Some players dunk the ball. This is when the player jumps high and places the ball directly in the basket.

Sometimes the ball misses the net. It may hit the **backboard**. It may bounce off the **rim**.

Anyone can catch the ball after a missed shot. When they do, it is a **rebound**.

Fast Fact!
Backboards are often made of very thick plastic.

14

16

Fouls and Free Throws

If you break the rules, the ref will call a **foul**. After a foul, a team may get to shoot **free throws**.

Fast Fact!
Refs blow their whistles to stop the game when a foul happens.

To shoot a free throw, you stand at the **free throw line**. Both teams wait for you to throw the ball. You focus on the basket. Then you take your shot.

If you make your free throw, you get one point. You might even get to shoot again. After your last free throw, everyone starts playing again.

Fast Fact!
Basketball games are split into halves. At halftime, the teams switch baskets.

19

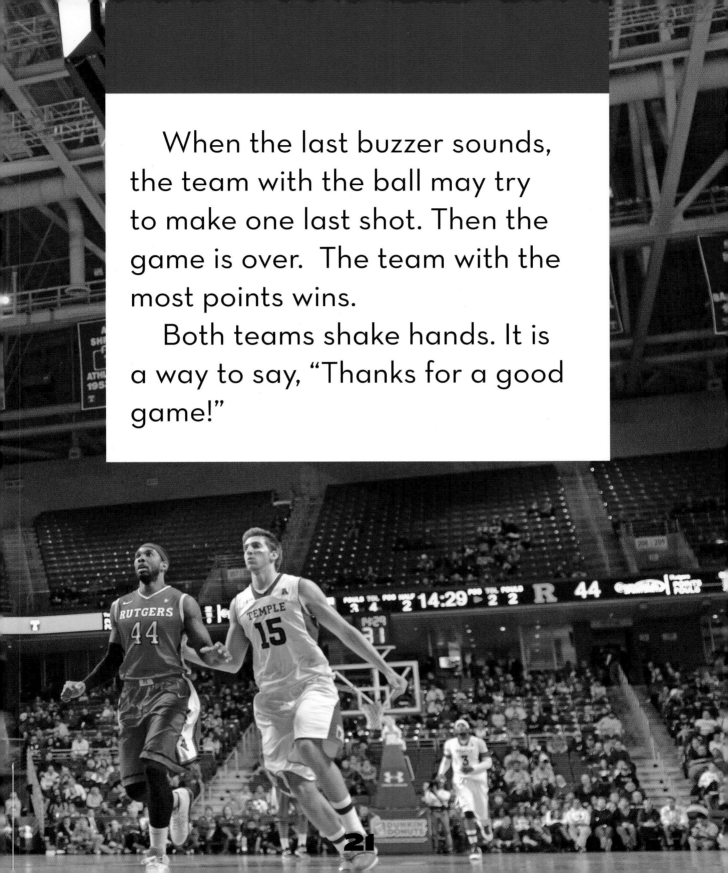

When the last buzzer sounds, the team with the ball may try to make one last shot. Then the game is over. The team with the most points wins.

Both teams shake hands. It is a way to say, "Thanks for a good game!"

Glossary

backboard (BAK-bord): A large, flat panel behind the basket. Players can bounce balls off the backboard and into the basket.

basket (BASS-ket): The rim and net that the basketball must go through to earn points. The word also means the act of getting the ball through the net.

dribbling (DRIB-ling): The way a player moves from place to place with a basketball. Players must bounce the ball with one hand the whole time they are running or walking.

foul (FOWL): An action that breaks the rules is called a foul.

free throw line (FREE THROH LINE): A line painted on the basketball court. You must stand behind it when shooting free throws.

free throws (FREE THROHZ): Shooting baskets while everyone else stands still. Free throws are awarded for fouls.

layup (LAY-up): A way to shoot a basketball on the run. The player holds the ball in one hand, jumps up with the opposite leg, and throws the ball while in the air.

net (NET): The net is the looped, open fabric that a team must drop the ball through.

pass (PASS): When one player throws or bounces the ball to another player it is called a pass.

rebound (REE-bownd): The act of catching the ball after it bounces off the backboard or rim. The word is also used for the bounce itself.

ref (REF): Referee. This is the person who makes sure all players follow the rules.

rim (RIM): The rim is the round frame that holds the basketball net open and in place.

steal (STEEL): A steal happens when the team that doesn't have the ball takes it away from the team with the ball.

tip-off (TIP-awff): The way a basketball game begins, where two players face each other while the referee holds the ball. When the referee throws the ball up high, each player tries to get the ball or hit it toward someone on his or her team.

To Learn More

In the Library

Campbell, Forest G., and Fred Ramen. *An Insider's Guide to Basketball*. New York: Rosen Central, 2015.

Hantula, Richard. *Science at Work in Basketball*. New York: Marshall Cavendish Benchmark, 2012.

Sports Illustrated for Kids, eds. *Sports Illustrated Kids Slam Dunk!: Top 10 Lists of Everything in Basketball*. New York, NY: Time Home Entertainment, 2014.

On the Web

Visit our Web site for links about basketball:
childsworld.com/links

Note to Parents, Teachers, and Librarians: We routinely verify our Web links to make sure they are safe and active sites. So encourage your readers to check them out!

Index

About the Author

Kara L. Laughlin is an artist and writer who lives in Virginia with her husband, three kids, two guinea pigs, and a dog. She is the author of two dozen nonfiction books for kids.